One Year.

Byron James

I wrote a lot in 2010-11. Let's just say that the emotional devastation of separation is fantastic at concentrating the mind in some ways while leaving you utterly adrift in others.

I wrote. I travelled. I did pretty much anything but work. It's ironic, it became impossible to focus the mind on working, but then writing got easier.

I learned how to meditate. I learned to slow down and to accept that working was not in and of itself a goal.

So, in a very real way I have to thank my estranged wife for the time I've spent on writing, travelling and generally changing my life from top to bottom. Here's to you love, I wouldn't have done it without you.

Byron

1
Weeds in the snow
The grey sky of the day
Salt underfoot

2
Springtime - sell the house
We go our separate ways
No more dreams of you

3
White afternoon sky
Lost for words in your presence
I remain silent

4
Dawn beaks - the new day
Still, nothing stirs in the cold.
The morning wood

5

In the morning wood
The bird in trembling hand
Struggles to be free

6

Winter - the cold house
It hurts just to look at you
Saturday morning

7

Today as before
Beside me - empty, dreamless
Your side of the bed

8

The bedside table
Strewn with coins and memories
That lie - forgotten

9
The changing season
These hands - worn with time and care
This slow betrayal

10
This old house - quiet
This bed - empty, these arms too
Words unspoken

11
A winter Friday
Sitting with an old friend
Life's music playing

12
The winter deep-freeze
Alone under the duvet
I miss your cold feet

13
You're a good man
That's what she said to me
Yet she left

14
Coffee with myself
Sounds of the house - waking up
Bitter aftertaste

15
Without reason to
I'm wondering where you are -
Who you are with now?

16
A bird on the wire
A dog in the park barks
Echoes in the cold

17
Coffee in bed
Alone with my thoughts
Waiting for the day

18
Winter's claws are sharp
Cold wind bites at the walls
The long darkness

19
Nighttime
The old house sighs in the wind
Winter's grip tightens

20
You won't believe this
I've come all this way alone
Just to forget you

21
I want to go home
To the comfort of my house
With all its noises

22
Words fail me
Coddled by the lies I've heard
I am brought to my knees

23
A table for one
Reflecting back on the day
Steaming tea in hand

24
Eyes closed -
Remembering your face,
the scent of your hair

25
Morning sun rising
Blindingly bright to the eyes
Warm on winter skin

26
The sounds of the house
Makes a music of its own
As I wait for sleep

27
Pain does go away
Not without leaving a mark
Memories remain

28
Sounds of distant crows
A January snow fall
This cold stinging wind

29

Bronte, our next stop.
In the gathering darkness
My path leads me home

30

The smell of coffee
The kitchen is mine, alone
Your footsteps are gone

31

I would hold you close
But this house is empty now
This bed is so cold

32

Thick snow falls quickly
The pine boughs become heavy
Silence rules the day

33
Coffee this morning
Like the sun in the winter
Weak and cold, again

34
Goodbye came today
And with a smile you left me
In the falling snow

35
Walking on eggshells,
Quietly licking our wounds.
Waiting for the sun.

36
We are gossamer.
Fleeting as the morning dew.
Embrace your time here.

37

Taste oblivion,
The ozone, sulphur stink of it.
Begging on your knees.

38

Cold lips meet cold lips,
hands warming one another,
frosty evening kiss.

39

Autumn foliage,
Now crushed and broken by snow
crocuses hiding.

40

Remain reticent.
Say nothing, do even less.
Forget her, move on.

41

This ancient creature,
old beyond time, beyond hope
still waits to be loved

42

Dogwood in the snow,
Sheltering the hope of spring.
Breath freezing in air.

43

The mouse in springtime.
Cautious, not venturing far,
for fear of the owl.

44

Slow motion death dance.
We circle around the truth.
This, our love - is dead.

45

Winter grass in snow
Lifeless, waving in the wind.
My love for you fades.

46

This dark forest path,
Urges us to go onwards,
Yet, leads us in circles.

47

The winter silence,
a muted memory now.
Distant crows all out.

48

This cup of coffee,
hot, satisfying, empty.
Like casual sex.

49

I feel your warm breath,
I smell the scent of your skin.
Pity, it's a dream.

50

This parade of souls,
bright, luminescent, alive.
I watch from shadows.

51

dorobouneko.
The sneaky cat from next door.
An unfaithful wife.

52

Night came creeping in.
Memories of you came too.
I turn off the light.

53

Thursday evening,
The two of us in the house,
walking on eggshells.

54

Winter rain, drumming,
cold room, cheerless and empty.
A fragile headache.

55

Death comes, sleek and chrome.
It never saw it coming,
the squirrel lies dead

56

this morning coffee
made for the ghost of our love,
I drink it alone

57
Here it comes again
that ragged, tearing west wind
full of knives and teeth

58
the night wind bellows
everything shrinks from its bite
shelter from the storm

59
What does it feel like,
roasting my heart on a stick?
will you eat it too?

60
Sanctimonious:
Showing your tits on Facebook,
then going to church

61

wind through naked boughs
winter strips away the warmth
the outline of life

62

The winter grasses
Broken in the freezing wind
Wave defiantly

63

Beneath the snow, cold
The crocus waits for the sun
dreaming away pain

64

Empty Sunday night
Snow falls, dog barks, marking time
The song of the house

65

The day wears onwards
I work - plagued by memory
This pain in my chest

66

In my own eyes
I cannot be a good man
for letting love die

67

When love has faded
the husk remains, haunting
This ghost is our own

68

When love has faded
the husk remains, haunting
This ghost is our own

69

Furious weather
Unpredictable as love
Cold as the night air

70

Cool shrouding mist
Bamboo groves wave slowly
A flock of crows

71

Morning fog - bamboo
One thousand steps uphill
Silence in the mist

72

Looking for you
In all the old places
The corners of the heart

73
The day slid by - quietly
Barely a word between us
Dying in silence

74
Approaching evening
Loud silences in this house
I retreat inward

75
At home yet alone
Her voice that of a ghost, hovers
I crawl into bed

76
This lonely evening
Tonight we dine on blood and aphorisms
Chewing over bones

77

There is no recourse
In her court of whispered lies
I stand convicted

78

"Sanctimonious."
First, you should get a mirror
Then look up the word.

79

Your adultery.
Actions not of my doing.
Your choices, alone.

80

Refrigerate me.
Best kept in a cold, dark place.
Canada will do.

81
What rough footsteps these?
Crushing crocus underfoot
to die in spring snow.

82
I'm ignoring you.
Morning in this quiet house.
Sound of closing door.

83
Consider for once,
your sanctimoniousness,
and adultery

84
in utter defeat
down hard on his bleeding knees
the phoenix will rise

85

Springtime buds in show
Her white cold grasp pushed away
The robins singing

86

This thin covering
all mere ash in the making
we treasure it now.

87

Heart, beating in air.
Flesh gone, ribcage ripped away.
Pounding pulse like drums.

88

Her dark lips kiss me.
The full warmth of her embrace.
Morning espresso.

89
a sucking blackness
a hole in the heart
where a life once was

90
Worn creaking old chair.
Floors that groan under footsteps.
I'll miss this old house.

91
Quiet evening.
Waiting here for the darkness.
Evening blooms, fragrant.

92
Crows calling at dawn.
Sounds of a distant train pass.
All threads that life weaves.

93
Bare maple, dawn sky.
Darkness gives way to daylight.
So passes sorrow.

94
I stand here, naked.
Without my armour, no words.
Take me as I am.

95
"You are a good man."
So you told me, then left.
Condemned by faint praise.

96
Snowy, winter path.
Walking alone, with out you.
Sadness is knowing.

97
Such a fragile thing.
A spider in the kitchen.
I leave it in peace.

98
These hands that knew love.
The house that they built for us.
No longer know you.

99
One thousand haiku.
Alight on this page, like birds.
Brush away the tear.

100
Your beautiful hands,
long, slender, strong.
No longer mine.

101

Pack this life away
In boxes and in darkness
Turn and lock the door

102

Painful silences
"I don't love you anymore."
That took 18 years.

103

Stepping cautiously
Walking the gossamer road
Waiting for the fall

104

Decades beat down hard
The strongest of us, humbled
Waiting for release

105
The pilgrim's long walk
Praying for what cannot be
Blood from bended knee

106
Cold mist, springtime air
no warmth from the absent sun
shiver in the rain

107
Nighttime's hushed echoes
Empty footsteps in the hall
The loneliest sound

108
Witless, bewildered
Betrayed by the one he loved
He trusts no one now

109

Smoke and ash, the past.
The fun and games are over.
Enough, no more lies.

110

words wander(loosely)[
Meanwhile an[array] of thoughts()]
Tramples(off) the page

111

Ten minutes ago {
I had no idea then
} but I know that now

112

Darkness held at bay
A thousand tiny, warm lights
Waiting out the storm

113
Thunder in the dark
Late night skies opening up
Feel the rain - feel it

114
Another night - rain
Steady drumming on the roof
Frigid soaking beat

115
[there] are sounds at night
[yet] they are ethereal
[gone] before being

116
"I'll sleep when I'm dead."
Or so the old saying goes
"…before then." I hope

117

Cold Monday morning
As gossamer, thoughts float by
Echoes of time passed

118

Snow on a spring day
Freezing winds that sting the eyes
No warmth anywhere

119

Cold wind on Sunday.
Words fly by but can't be caught
Birds on harried wing

120

Wind tearing at trees
steady patter of the rain
just one heart beating

121
"coffee for one please…"
Another morning alone
A cold April rain

122
Amongst silent reeds
Frog song fills the morning air
Ripples in the pool

123
One warm August day
when our paths no longer crossed
Who left? Who's leaving?

124
crepuscular life
rabbits fighting on the lawn
owl in the tree

125

Silently hands grasp
Echo of a distant fear
The smell of metal

126

The world grows colder
As the silences expand
Politely lying.

127

In the darkened house
The silence becomes louder
Waiting for the dawn

128

Amid winter's leaves
the cardinal forages
spring has arrived here

129
Gathering dark dogs
Stalking in slow wide circles
I lie down, prepared

130
Worlds become undone
Spiraling particle mass
Reinventing life

131
The day is done now
alone in the house, I write
alone in the house

132
As with any journey
Each new day moves us apart
living separate lives

133
I loved coming home,
Because, I knew you'd be there
Two solitudes

134
Cold springtime sunset
Slow gathering of shadows
Crows in the distance

135
A foggy morning.
Red-winged blackbirds in the mist.
The sounds of springtime.

136
eyes that sting burn
gasping for air and release
we swim, dissolving

137
Sitting alone here.
Knowing you're sleeping downstairs
Living, separately.

138
Spring sun through maples.
The quiet hush of the house.
The taste of coffee.

139
I want more of less
and a great deal less of more
not so much to ask

140
love - don't make me laugh
too many write about love
too few about life

141
rainy sunday morn
company in a coffee cup
headache on the rise

142
a heart on his sleeve
probably not his own though
he's such a faker

143
exhaustion takes him
brought to his wobbling knees
he bows down - silent

144
serenely quiet
a day with only birdsong
music while I write

145
a moment alone
has turned into a whole year
his heart grows more numb

146
coffee goes with rain
more so this morning it seems
deep breath - let it pass

147
hot, fresh espresso
dried pitted dates and burfi
missing - your laughter

148
let's write about love
whisper me a pretty lie
then kiss me deeply

149
which way is forward?
on this goat path through the hills
following instinct

150
wake to a new day
say a prayer for the living
give thanks to the dead

151
Hills beset with stars
Shining under velvet skies
Breathe in the night air

152
village in the mist
here on a distant hilltop
reach out - touch the clouds

153
Crows call in the mist
Bamboo waving in the breeze
Breathe in slowly - wait

154
sunshine warms green grass
children laughing as they run
day begins anew

155
stone cold mug of tea
cold, comfortless and bitter
like her company

156
on a sky blue day
i would see you laugh again
the wind in your hair

157
Love, life, love of life
sadness and beauty are yours
the threads that life weaves

158
misty mountain grove
standing as a boy in awe
recalling the rain

159
these silent pathways
through memory and heartbreak
gently faded love

160
consider her ways
her hands as they hold a book
her eyes when you talk

161
delicate moments
the salty taste of our words
senses reaching out

162
hearts too cold to save
faltering footsteps stagger
love it seems - dies here

163
gentle wind sings soft
the afternoon winds slowly down
sitting without you

164
blithely onwards now
these poetic perversions
sex without touching

165

whispers in her ear
the love that you hide away
is love for yourself

166

Her tenuous life
A delicate beating heart
Held in trembling hands

167

Early evening
Slow, gentle drifting, eyes closed
Descend into sleep

168

Hands that shake and sweat
A million worries circle
Close the door and sleep

169
Would like to nap now,
No girlfriend to snuggle with.
Make tea, watch the rain.

170
Sleep deprived Tuesday
Staggering through the haze of work
Watching the damned clock

171
Misty spring morning
Magnolia in full bloom
I pause, then make tea

172
We walk together
Melancholia and I
Her cold, distant voice

173

Here on this mountain
In the delicate stillness
We stand, touching clouds

174

Standing, wrapped in cloud
for a moment time stands still
The sound of the wind

175

Dampness wrapped in cold
Skies above, flat, pale, rainy grey.
Winter holds on still

176

Morning without you
An unbearable coldness
Early morning rain

177
A long, cold, damp spring
This being and nothingness
Blossoms in the ice

178
Heavy eyelids fall
Rebelliously, thoughts remain
Write this down, then sleep

179
Quiet May evening
Missing your warm company
Not for the last time

180
Spent, waiting for sleep.
Reeling from the day's efforts.
Wanting to␣be held.

181
Another evening
Haunted by this empty house
Making tea for one

182
Dust slowly settles,
released from the long pursuit.
A distant thunder.

183
Telling pretty lies
She wandered away with him.
That too was a lie

184
Travelling alone
Roads rise and take you away.
We wave as you go.

185
She says she's empty,
Her heart too tired to cry.
She never told him.

186
she arose softly
her footsteps made not a sound
the morning she left

187
A life for a life.
Reflect on what has been won.
Revenge is fleeting.

188
Dreamily blinking
Woolgathering weariness
Silent apathy

189

Cold comfortless rain
Days passing in slow silence
More that can be known

190

An afternoon nap
May day rainy afternoon
Lone crow's rasping call

191

I have a dark side
it comes out to play at night
waxing poetic

192

the scent of your hair
it's still here in the pillow
though your warmth is gone

193
I'd like to have you
right on the tip of my tongue
so I can taste you

194
lay your head down here
close your eyes and sigh gently
let me read to you

195
his dry plaster heart
ceased its beating long ago
a heart for hearts sake

196
We have to go now
We should've left long ago
Our time is over

197
waiting for daybreak
haunted by yesterday's ghosts
hovering softly

198
sleep settles softly
my eyes fight to stay open
a losing battle

199
I want a shoulder
and maybe a warm, soft lap.
someone to read to

200
chorus of dogs bark
pale evening sky hung with cloud
sitting in the dark

201
a persistent ache
a dull throb - deep in the chest
that time will not heal

202
could we just lay here
my head on your warm, soft breast?
our fingers entwined

203
birdsong and traffic
awake! and greet the new day
gently chiding me

204
if you give your heart
include the barbecue sauce
and bring some napkins

205
if you give your heart
include the barbecue sauce
and bring some napkins

206
you don't love me, so
I leave you here like this
to cry for nothing

207
she gave him diamonds
he gave her a string of pearls
and then they showered

208
her warm embrace
the slow poison of her kiss
she is poetry

209
poetry is
those things you could never say
when the time was right

210
he ran out of words
his well has run dry again
leaving worms and mud

211
a quiet breath
in a still quieter house
listening for her

212
making coffee
I remember her hands
the way they felt

213
her footsteps are gone
leaving the house empty
her heart gone missing

214
his heart did tricks
vanishing from time to time
not leaving notes

215
cold comfort
and a hot cup of coffee
so, where to from here?

216
evenings were harder
the walls closed in as it came
memories pressed down

217
the trouble with her
is that she tastes like more
back to the bedroom

218
the dark of night
velvet cool and rainy
wraps around our eyes

219
morning light weak - cold
no comfort in this coffee
sitting here alone

220
the whir of the fan
that cool and steady white-noise
invites me to sleep

221
a parting of ways
life doesn't get much harder
pathways through the mist

222
days end weariness
weighs heavy on hands and mind
tripping on my words

223
I am quite empty
devoid of all intention
I wander aimless

224
You left me empty
worse off than I was before
it wasn't worth it

225
we remain undone
ever a work in progress
will you walk with me?

226
a storm is coming
I stopped thinking of my pain
the sound of raindrops

227
this fire went out
the steady cold rain doused it
ending up so cold

228
a welcome respite
aching hearts hold warm teacups
quiet friendly words

229
burning sun above
we seek the cool dark of shade
waiting for moonrise

230
these ash illusions
not a living thing in sight
memories burning

231
one day like the next
ending with no one to hold
no one to talk with

232
the traveler stops
his back freed from his troubles
waiting for the night

233
undone by her hands
unwound, unbound and unkissed
yes, children - love dies

234
I wish I weren't here
horizons are calling me
and i am alone

235
the end beginning
ashes left from burning love
sunshine through the dust

236
dappled morning sun
pours across my darkened room
not making a sound

237
another morning
another cup of coffee
another (alone)

238
harsh morning wakeup
birdsong and writing - breakfast
me and me - alone

239
wishing you where here
naked, dreaming, break of day
to love and be loved

240
asleep and dreaming
wrapped around your warm body
only it's not true

241
they're drawn together
from that first kiss to the last
sweet shuddering sigh

242
a quiet moment
where does the morning find you?
enrobed in your thoughts?

243
a tiny red line
runs off to my horizon
glowing in the sun

244
five hours of sleep
coffee isn't going to help
where are you now, love?

245
noises from the park
t-shirt and my boxer shorts
write the morning down

246
treasured above all
her tireless beating heart
within fortress walls

247
a new day begins
only my footsteps in the house
black coffee - alone

248
this house is too dark
exhausted from not sleeping
all I see are ghosts

249

sleep just won't come home
the scent of roses at night
a warm summer wind

250

silence (feel/taste/know/hate/love/smell) silence
mute footsteps in the old house
(here/there) love (lays/falls/rests)
(silent/dusty/rotting) - dead

251

borne in on the wind
where does the evening find you?
whose bed are you in?

252

He remains silent
Afraid of the rejection
watching life pass by

253
I really (like/dig) her
How is this supposed to work?
(worship from afar)

254
He staggers a bit
Not because he's been drinking
Bullshit is heavy

255
She made it quite clear
Telling him she loved someone
Someone else, that is

256
(warm/cool) (winter/summer)) (calm/wind) (blows/sighs)
a strand of (her/your) hair (waving/blowing)
(my/your) eyes deceive (you/me)

257
words fail me just now
watching the moth and the flame
knowing how it ends

258
heart and hands - empty
has all this love been for naught?
kneeling in defeat

259
the dream of a child
laughter, sandboxes, sunlight
these we never lose

260
tread lightly this path
keep yourself for yourself
giving as given

261

every word he wrote
muted - fell on deafened ears
silence wins again

262

siren in the night
motorcycle rattles by
sounds that darkness makes

263

Oh, I love the night.
Wrapped in it's dark arms I dream
It loves me deeply

264

a walk after dark
this summer moon horizon
he shares with no one

265
see the peacock strut
displaying his bright plumage
hiding the chicken

266
she held me once - warm
"you know your way around me"
it wasn't enough

267
here, without the dream
a blind eye seeking the path
guided by sheer will

268
quietly resigned
to a day without feeling
step into the void

269
my pen is empty
words collide with no meaning
I stare at my hands

270
(whispers to himself)
"maybe one day I'll know love."
(if I'm not dead first)

271
Tuesday is so slow
Empty minutes marking time
weak and useless hands

272
Cyan - kinda blue
there is no warmth in the sun
a cold wind blowing

273
today is so thin
held together in this fog
blinded - wandering

274
frost on her cold lips
"fundamentals can't be changed"
unredeemable

275
there's so little left
perhaps enough to stand on
the void - underfoot

276
fields ablaze - red skies
meadowlarks die in the smoke
their song now silenced

277
willingly drifting
senses let go of the world
rising on the tide

278
semi-lucid state
folding time sideways and down
killing memories

279
wind in the maple
noises from an empty house
that was once a home

280
seagull's ceaseless cry
time and tide wash through this house
your ghost still lingers

281
seething resentment
drawn out over sharp silence
eviscerate trust

282
a murder of crows
their rough call - brash unceasing
a carrion feast

283
what rough beast is this
with ragged hair and torn limbs
lays down - wanting you

284
time fell about them
legions stood silent - waiting
their eyes closed in prayer

285
I drifted away
adrift on a sea of thoughts
seeking no shelter

286
words can't capture you
you dance on a line through time
my quill has run dry

287
Our separation
as we dissolve into air
love lies bleeding out

288
these things - like her love
once a treasured possession
to be disposed of

289
entwined around him
serpentine memories wait
hunting for their prey

290
fear - cold and distant
holding their tongues prisoner
hands that never touch

291
a night full of sleep
waking to a cool, bright dawn
alone and quiet

292
latte and sunshine
the only warmth in my day
bed was too damned cold

293

cold morning coffee
cold and unmade empty bed
cold weekend coming

294

she loves who she will
her body is a temple
her mind is her own

295

warm dappled sunshine
cafe-hopping bon vivant
no cares for the day

296

cafe afternoon
laughter, sunshine, clinking ice
lunchtime crowd leaving

297
pervasive silence
heavy, thick with resentment
echoes in the void

298
despite best efforts
your dogmatic acumen
makes me want to laugh

299
he watches her eyes
she sees the world in a line
captured in the ink

300
he stops to reflect
wondering if he loved her
a silent moment

301
to love is to lose
to open one's heart to pain
knowing it will come

302
"time waits for no man."
"but what if you're still a boy?"
"shut up. no questions."

303
spilling words not blood
he staggers under the truth
he is alone now

304
slow moving fingers
picking their way through the words
blind to time and space

305
he finds no warmth
no strength in the summer sun
frozen to the core

306
his frost covered heart
beating behind bony walls
longing for the sun

307
Four in the morning
wandering this empty house
echoes of the past

308
clouds drifting slowly
a velvet summer nighttime
wanting to believe

309

ethereal soul

she is traced in but a line

he cannot follow

310

hot June afternoon

manky old cat in the yard

squirrel waits on the fence

311

swollen by his pride

he no longer fits through doors

alone in his room

312

yesterday - it was

he wrote of such happiness

fleeting will-o'-wisp

313
to sleep without dreams
little death that comes slowly
into darkness go

314
the adulteress
years of selfishness in tow
ruin in her wake

315
crash and burn fucker
molten flesh among the flames
pain you won't forget

316
consider the reed
too proud to bend in the wind
broken - it falls down

317

under the hammer
we are tempered by the fire
hard and cold as steel

318

morning. coffee. toast.
dog out - barking in the yard
counting down minutes

319

wake me from this dream
if indeed a dream it is
I can't find my way home

320

cool welcoming shade
shelter from the burning sun
Shiva still dances

321
gentle sigh of wind
bamboo sways to a rhythm
tracing the warm curve

322
string the strongest bow
nock the red arrow and draw
hunting to kill love

323
naked and the nude
subliminal or sublime
poetry and words

324
death remains silent
indifferent to his wishes
a cold tear rising

325
to have and to hold
to be had and to be held
repeat as needed

326
he waits, wondering
myriad gossamer thoughts
behind his closed eyes

327
not for words alone
a lover, friend, traveler
someone to be with

328
barefoot down the stairs
wooden floor creaking softly
I'll miss this old house

329
silly old wanker
writing poems to no one
sitting in the dark

330
coffee is calling
numb, sleepy nerve endings wake
dull fingers writing

331
wake up - roll over
feel for you in the cold sheets
you were never here

332
writers feed on pain
poets make lousy lovers
still - it's a lifestyle

333
my eyes wide open
yet I fail to see it all
this restless motion

334
a sip of coffee
strong and bitter on my tongue
the last words spoken

335
just my own breathing
all traces of you are gone
emptiness observed

336
hunger hunts him down
sleepless, lidless eyes observe
the consuming soul

337
her delicate feet
her cold toes in the morning
dancing through the house

338
another day here
crows call, coffee brews, I write
Saturday morning

339
endless labours lost
over grown with time and age
the silent garden

340
when tomorrow came
there was still no love to hold
another cold day

341
To be by the sea.
the scent of waves in the air
watching the tides roll

342
is it really love?
it's just too easy to say.
much harder to prove

343
my hand on your breast
last time I felt a heart beat
I don't recall now

344
the miles travelled
moving images in time
dust under my feet

345
she's gone, there's silence
her footsteps, the air she stirred
settling silence

346
there is, in this place
penetrating silences
oppressive quiet

347
his threadbare spirit
worn by time, riddled with holes
yearns for her soft touch

348
we danced in the rain
the band played on through the storm
we laughed, kissed and splashed

349
the naked poet
writing in his darkened loft
sweating out the words

350
night street soaked in rain
the sheets have all been kicked off
air too thick to breathe

351
I struggle for words
a drowning man lost at sea
his last sight, the sky

352
afternoon coffee
black, bitter, tasting of ash
nighttime, in a cup

353
dry summer grass sways
the burning heat of midday
cicada chorus

354
she watched me falling
covered in muck and crawling
I watched her walk off

355
you float - a mirage
between death and the dreaming
outside of my reach

356
I laughed at myself
trapped inside this flesh and blood
decoding the world

357
chaotic spinning
and the dance of ideas
leaves the heart aching

358
finding 'le mot juste'
telling it like we see it
nude but not naked

359
[embrace the sunshine]
(today happens only once)
(making memories)

360
wake in a stupor
fumble for the alarm clock
knowing I'm alone

361
cold frost encrusted
emptiness squeezes his heart
air from empty lungs

362
blackened lungs and heart
burnt fingertips smoldering
my demons abound

363
reflect on the loss
they no longer stand with us
we bury our dead

364
two ghosts roamed the house
separation and divorce
it was dark today

[I'll get trough this, watch]
[bruised, bloodied and on one knee]
[unbowed, unbroken]

365
she removes her clothes
standing naked, trembling
seeking acceptance

Afterword

My thanks to my good friend and editor Hannah Cai, who patiently selected the work, argued for or against various pieces and generally put up with my moods throughout the process of working on the book.

www.ingramcontent.com/pod-product-compliance
Lightning Source LLC
Chambersburg PA
CBHW072010090426
42734CB00033B/2416